SPOKES FROM THE WHEEL OF LIFE

To Theresa,

Enjoy these poems
& hope that some
inspire you!
With thanks

Ian

JM Scott

Published under licence by Brown Dog Books and
The Self-Publishing Partnership Ltd, 10b Greenway Farm, Bath Rd,
Wick, nr. Bath BS30 5RL

www.selfpublishingpartnership.co.uk

ISBN printed book: 978-1-83952-597-1
ISBN e-book: 978-1-83952-598-8

Cover design by Kevin Rylands
Internal design by Andrew Easton

Printed and bound in the UK

This book is printed on FSC® certified paper

MIX
Paper | Supporting
responsible forestry
FSC
www.fsc.org   FSC® C013604

SPOKES FROM THE WHEEL OF LIFE

J A SCOTT

BROWN
DOG
BOOKS

Acknowledgements

For my husband, son, family and friends, who have
endured my poetic ramblings for longer than I can
remember and for my parents and two brothers who
contributed to my resilience and sense of humour when
growing up. For my six wonderful grandchildren who, I
hope, may read my poetry one day.

Last but not least, for my clients who have inspired and
shown me the similarities between us all, regardless of
any differences.

Foreword

I have enjoyed reading poetry all of my life. I was born in Essex where I spent much of my life until 2008, when I relocated to Suffolk.

I have had many poems published in a local newspaper over 10 years, one printed in This England Calendar 2020 and several on the NHS mental health website for World Mental Health Day. I have, through my work as a psychotherapist in the NHS, been inspired by human beings' ability to heal from painful experiences through their own resilience and courage, particularly when using creative methods like poetry, music, craft and art as a media to express emotions where conversational words can't be found.

My own experiences of growing up in a working-class home, being a single parent and encountering (as we all do) life-changing events and personal tragedies, have inspired me to write this collection of poetry mostly about my observations of life, loss and adjustment. Some you may find to be 'clichéd' and a little 'tongue in cheek' with regard to the way British people view the weather, holidays and other life experiences, but this commonality means they may resonate with you and your experience of life too.

This book of reflective poetry hopes to inspire you as the reader, so that you too, may relate to it and find it, in some way, healing, amusing and enlightening.

Contents

Reflective

Most of us can remember and imagine. There might be moments that bring warmth to our hearts, reminiscing on what life could be like, what life is like now and what it once was. Here are some poems that have been sparked by moments of inspiration and memories.

Do You My Friend Remember?

Do you, my friend, remember,
Your friends about that age,
When we danced around our handbags,
As that was all the rage?

When pop icons were our heroes,
And we took to the floor to dance,
When we boogied to the hits that week,
And we all got lost in trance.

When we were all such pretty things,
When our days lasted forever,
When these were just the golden years,
And we all joined in together.

When we were all the young ones,
Just starting out, beginners,
It was all about the fashion,
And burgers over dinners.

When late nights weren't for lightweights,
When we queued at Ali Baba's,
For those dodgy filled big kebabs,
Then went home to raid the larders.

When we missed the 251 bus,
Back to our home address,
Walked the six miles homeward,
And arrived a shocking mess.

When we crept inside the front door,
Stumbling quietly up the stair,
Between each creaky floorboard,
Our sleeping parents unaware.

When we clambered into bed then,
With our head a spinning round,
We'd vow this was the last time,
Till next Saturday came around.

Choices

So many choices in this life,
Too many paths to take,
So many roads where we can go,
Too many rules to break.

Life lies before us, with its strange twists and turns,
And the challenges we face, help us grow.
It's the wisdom that we gain, when we face what is hard,
And we learn how to cope as we go.

It's sometimes so hard when our lives get so tough,
And the routes that we chose, all goes wrong,
But it's not always for our choosing and it doesn't mean we're losing,
Just keep your chin up, try again and be strong.

When the road seems curved and rocky and you feel you're alone,
Hold your hand out to another who'll be there,
There's no shame in admitting, you really feel like quitting,
When it seems deep in your soul that they don't care.

For nothing is forever, troubles come and go each day,
And you know you'll overcome them and you'll then,
Pick up the broken part of your unhappy, saddened heart
Dust yourself off, leave the past and start again.

What If?

What if I were to wake up,
One hundred years from now?
What would life then look like?
It's hard to imagine how.

Would we need the cars we own?
Or would travel be so fast?
Would the sky be filled with flying cars,
That we'd see zooming past?

Would food be bought as powder,
Delivered to our door?
Free from all known chemicals,
And nothing less than raw.

And how about relationships
That we'd no longer need?
When producing custom babies,
Bought online in packet seed.

School and education,
They'll be no human tutors,
Robots without emotions,
With no classroom, just computers.

And money that would be no more,
When the blinking of our eye,
Would give us what we need each day,
No more we'd need Wi-Fi.

But then about world conflict,
Would they still fight for their cause?
Or would they believe in nothing,
So, there'd be no more wars?

Although we'll never know all this,
In our minds, we can create,
A brand-new future filled with things,
That nothing can abate.

For whatever future lies ahead,
We've laid down our foundation,
So those who tread after we've gone,
Can build a new creation.

Think Twice

Think twice before you judge them,
With tattoos and slang slung voices.
With their children with no father
And others, with no choices,

Don't ignore them like you seem to,
With disapproving, downturned eyes
With your riches that define you
And distaste you can't disguise.

As you judge with no reason but fortune,
To negate those who don't have such charm,
There's within all those that repel you,
A strength that with do you no harm.

Why not try with your heart to give friendship?
After all we're the same but for wealth,
No one knows after all what befalls us,
Unemployment, loss, bad health.

So next time when you catch yourself feeling
That you're grander than those who have less,
Just check in on that judge deep inside you,
And remember it's just luck that you're blessed.

Light Up the Sky

Light up the sky,
With a glow of love tonight,
Cease war and hate
And behold all that is right.

Join hands together,
Regardless of belief,
With joy and acceptance
And relieve us from the grief.

Be who you are
Suspending judgements vast.
Live for each other
And bury what is past.

Believe your religion,
But impose it not on us.
The idea that it's only yours,
That brings such joy and love.

Postpone all your egos,
That validate your reasons,
Depriving others living out,
The remainder of their seasons.

Not just for one day only,
Be the person you were born,
Free from prejudice and hate,
Before the purpose of your dawn.

For if there is a judge out there,
When we have left this land so vast,
How on earth will justification stand,
When your day becomes your last?

So, think before you act so quick
Deter from callous acts,
And live in peace upon this earth.
Your beliefs are not the facts.

Today

Today I walked along the beach,
Just barefoot in the sand,
I felt the breeze upon my face,
And marvelled at this land.

I thought about how wonderful,
This moment was right here,
How beautiful the sky and sea,
Was at this time of the year.

I could have been just anywhere,
Right there upon the beach,
If I had not known where I was,
In countries out of reach.

For time is short so every day,
There's something here to capture,
In all the days upon this earth,
These moments of pure rapture.

So, take the moment in your hands,
And leave behind all worry,
There's nothing more than what is here
No need to fret or hurry.

For life goes on no matter what,
And each day is there to treasure.
Keep with the moment, seize the day
In sadness, joy or pleasure.

Pebbles on the Beach

Pebbles on the beach,
What words if you could speak,
Of a billion years of times past gone,
With weathers wild and bleak.

Pebbles on the beach,
How many feet have stood,
Of soldiers clad in armoured suits,
Where worn out feet have trod.

Pebbles on the beach,
A part of this big land,
Your journey spans so long it seems,
These rocks where winds have fanned.

Pebbles so unique,
Worn by the wrath of oceans,
Their million tales of life now gone,
With absence of emotion.

Pebbles on the beach,
Your surfaces unique,
Yet like them all such big and small,
Us humans go to seek.

Pebbles there are plenty,
In millions unlike gold,
All free for us to hold in hands,
Not stored till they are old

Pebbles on the beach,
Hold stories of these seas,
Basking briefly, beauty sweet,
Then back to sea released.

Moments

As each moment ticks on by,
Through hours of our day,
Our minds are often somewhere else,
With being led astray.

Spinning in directions,
Scrutinising minute flaws,
Our busy brains find spotlights,
At every open door.

Yet moments can be lost like this,
Each moment missed in time,
Worrying over what is next,
Wasted seconds so sublime.

Time cannot be captured,
Locked up, or put away,
It really is just here for now,
This moment of today.

So, when you're chasing life around,
And your head is all about,
Remember that you're missing much,
Mind and body all worn out.

Enjoy this time, this time is yours,
Let go of fret and woe,
For moments flash before our eyes,
Faster than you know.

Our Children

Children they will grow so fast,
Before we know it, it is past,
Childish pranks, bad behaviour,
Fly on past so we should savour.

Supermarket tantrums,
Dirty faces,
Always put us,
Through our paces.

Grubby hands,
On clean tables,
Reading stories,
Poems, fables.

When time's against us,
Patience tested
Peace forgotten,
No one's rested.

When we're tired,
In a muddle,
Embracing arms,
Demand a cuddle.

Not easy when,
It's all full on,
Before you blink,
It will be gone.

Relish all,
That these days bring,
Release the throttle,
Dance and sing.

Enjoy the moment,
That's all we need,
When our children,
We do feed.

As this time,
Will soon be ended,
When broken windows,
Will be mended

No time for stress,
Relentless worry,
Seize the moment,
Stop the hurry.

Time's so short,
Too short for fretting,
No point in looking back,
Regretting.

Nineteen Sixty

Back in nineteen sixty, making mud pies,
Mums were thrifty.
Family values, post-war rations,
Less concerned with latest fashions.

No extra helpings were to give,
In those days, we ate to live.
Even bath time was a chore,
Instead our faces scrubbed so raw.

In the kitchen, from the wash bowls,
Multitasked for kneading bread rolls,
Playing outside with others freely,
Off-ground touch, handstands and wheelies.

Money used for basic need,
Roof over head, mouths to feed,
Paying debts, so uncertain,
Hide from tally man, behind curtain.

Nostalgia being a reckoning force,
Looking back, we think of course,
All those simple, carefree days,
We were poor and so unphased.

Hardships that were far from brilliant
Nourished souls, to stand resilient.

What is a Dad?

A man who is there for you,
He may not have made you,
But he doesn't forsake you,
He doesn't have to look like you,
But he may cook for you,
Is there to hug you,
Even when you're grown,
He knows it's tough when you feel alone,
He can rough and tumble,
Complain at times and grumble,
Give you his listening ear,
When life gets you down,
And be the voice of reason,
When all you can find is a frown,
Yes, these things and more are what makes a dad.
Yet sometimes it's so sad,
Because for whatever reason,
They weren't or can't be there,
Maybe they were taken too young,
It just doesn't seem fair,
They were, and still are, our dads,
There's always a reason,
Though at times it's hard to comprehend,
And our heart sometimes can't mend,
So, treasure our dads while they're with us and,
Take from them the wisdom they give us,
For life is not forever,
Cherish those moments together.

Mum's Cake

I wish you could bake me a cake Mum,
The way you did back then,
When ingredients were all bought loose,
And I was only ten.

When butterfly cakes,
And lemon curd tarts,
Were only made by hand,
Compared to the ones sold down the shops,
Your cakes were somewhat grand.

Yes, I wish you could bake me a cake Mum,
All deliciously fluffy and light,
And topped with the freshest cream,
That you whipped with your hands all night.

But all I can do is dream now Mum,
For now, you're no longer here,
As I reminisce of your hug and kiss,
knowing you'll not appear.

For these memories stay within me,
When I think, and imagine you there,
For all that you were and all that you are,
There's just nothing that can compare.

So, until such time that we meet again,
I'll just remember those days in my mind,
For though you can't bake me those cakes now Mum,
In my memory, you still shine.

For with every passing thought I have,
Each vision of how it was then,
You'll live forever in my thoughts Mum,
And be with me once again.

Postcards

We didn't need a holiday,
To send them to our friends,
Posting from our local town,
From Clacton and Southend.

Trafalgar Square, Old Kent Road,
The Taj Mahal and China,
They really were all so unique,
Like snowflakes and bone china.

The saucy ones, the cheeky ones,
That made our aunties squeal.
The ones with dogs with wobbly eyes,
Always so surreal.

Adorning racks in seaside towns,
In post offices and shops,
But rarely feel the joy of when,
They dropped upon our mats.

We loved to get them in the post,

These written works of art,

Unlike communication now,

It went right to the heart.

So, let's all get a writing,

And surprise our friends back home.

Forward them a postcard,

So, they don't feel alone.

For the written word and all it's worth,

When sent to those we care,

Will bring a smile to all your friends,

When wishing they were there!

Parents

They're not perfect you know,
They made us, me and you,
Brought us into this big world,
Maybe, without a clue,

That children need a guiding hand,
A mentor, nurse and friend
To teach us how to live our lives,
Right to the very end.

There are times that we forget that,
Our parents are the same,
As the children they gave life to,
And we look to them to blame

The mistakes that we all make at times,
The pathways that we take,
Dwelling on past hurts and pains.
Our lives we do forsake

And yet, parents are just human,

Just like you and me,

With loaded insecurities,

Although it's hard to see.

So, while our lives may not turn out,

The way we wanted to,

Accept that while we blame them,

That, they're imperfect too.

Self-care

Here are a few poems that are personal to me, and which may resonate with you.

Self-care and healing can be found through writing about your experiences and reflections in times of trouble and stress.

Listen

Do you really listen,
I mean do you really hear?
To another's troubles,
Do you? Really loud and clear?

Usually that's not the case,
When those issues of your own,
Block out the sound while you go on,
With problems you do moan,

Do you really hear the pain,
That's in the words of friends?
That say 'please just hear me out'
With no fixing or amends.

Or do you spout before they've done,
With reminders of your life?
And so, rush on disinterested,
Cutting sharply with your verbal knife.

Yet if we truly listen,
Give others our attention,
While putting our own needs aside,
When our own we do not mention.

Just like a gift,
With no other cost but time,
Will heal much more than butting in,
With 'what's mine'

So, next time when you meet a friend,
Who's telling you their woes,
Just check in on your own stuff,
And store away like clothes.

For gifts are not just parcels,
Adorned in fancy wrap,
The best gift you can offer,
Is the one that seals your verbal trap.

Being Mindful

Being still's not easy,
In our big and busy day,
The worries that you cannot change,
Are getting in the way.

Problems that cannot be solved,
Your head feels so confused.
Dwelling on what's long since gone,
Does nothing to diffuse.

Yet when our minds are quietly still,
Just being in the now,
The busyness that's in your mind,
You'll notice and allow.

The worries, thoughts, the critical voice,
The anguish and the pain,
Your mind can just be curious,
And bring it back again.

This task will not be easy,
So, try it and be kind,
Once day it may surprise you,
The workings of your mind.

For every time that you arrive,
At this moment you are in,
Is one precious moment that you'll have back,
To then begin again.

Trauma

Your steps slow and furtive
Your actions so subdued
The walls you'd built around yourself
That no others heard or viewed

Your senses sharp and heightened
Reacting to small cues
Kept memories lingering in your head
No others heard your news

Self-protection served its purpose
Of course, and that made sense
But little did you know that
It was all in the past tense

Relief it was short lived, in fact
The price that was to pay
Was that years had passed before you
With you not living in today

So, walls built strong like concrete
Impermeable to most
Restricted you so badly
With the past a haunting ghost

Those dreams seemed like reality
Like you were still right there
The terror you experienced then again
Was unjust and unfair

In later years through therapy
A chance to start again
Each gentle step to live once more
Crawling gently from your den

Putting back the chaos
Running wild inside your head
Gave you strength to start to live
And deal with all the dread

Then peace came there to greet you
Those memories stored away
No more you're trapped within your walls
You're living in today.

Burn Out

Keep the pedals turning,
Within the cogs inside your mind,
Staying late to get it done,
With solutions that you find.

Skipping lunch time after time,
The weight drops from your thighs.
Taking lows throughout the day,
Foregoing all the highs.

Deadlines falling on your lap,
Increasingly unmet,
As pressure stored inside your head,
Follows you to bed.

Zombie-like you carry on,
While functions die like flowers.
No nutrients to find respite,
As you wake from early hours.

Those friends you have they tell you now,

You should have seen it coming,

Dripping like a faulty tap,

From the lifestyle you are running.

What's the point you ask yourself,

Brain/body link is failing.

Every organ under strain,

Slowly feel it ailing.

Mind's a fog, mistakes the norm,

Your voice inside is saying,

You've done it wrong, you're such fool,

Your patience starts a fraying.

But still you're blind to all the signs,

Your hamster wheel keeps turning,

One day you'll wake, jump from the wheel,

Before your feet start burning!

Love, Life & Loss

Most of us have known what it is like to love and to have been loved and as part of this, comes the pain of eventual loss through death, illness or separation. Recalling these times and about life in general within poetic form may also resonate in you, providing wisdom, healing and humour.

Patience

Patience waits for everyone,
Patience rarely fails,
Patience conquers everything,
That impatience so derails.

Waiting for each error,
Of human fallibility,
Patience always takes account,
The nature of fragility.

Yet patience wears thin on the ground,
When run ragged, tired and toiled,
When fractiousness and harsh strong words,
Leave emotions so embroiled.

And when patience dims our sparkling light,
With its edges frayed and tattered,
Step back with cautiousness and see,
That patience really mattered.

For if we were in shoes they trod,
And saw each other's struggle,
Maybe we'd be more inclined,
To be patient with their muddle.

Grudges

Grudges linger far too long,
Dwelling on what's right and wrong,
Seeping into hearts and mind,
Living in our heads they find,

Linger longer, eating in,
Grudges stay in minds within,
Prisoners of your private choice,
Bearing grudges with no voice,

Miscommunication errors,
Fill the head with mini terrors,
Creeping in the dead of night,
Stirring from the sleep we fight.

Weighing down so heavy-hearted,
Authenticity departed,
Forgotten all of your own needs,
As grudges grow and tension feeds.

Grudges uselessly are spent,
On resentments never seen or vent,
Pressure cooker boiling dry,
Emotions steam like trains gone by.

Wasted on past hurt and pains,
Do nothing for what can't be changed,
Eaten up, yet still malnourished,
Grudges like poison weeds they flourish.

There's a Play That You're In

There's a play that you're in, it's your life,
There are so many parts that you're in,
Changing roles as you go through the scenes,
Reaching out, chasing stars and your dreams.

There are parts that you play that are hard,
Those that test you beyond what seems real,
But you go on with stage fright and get through,
Even though this is not what you feel.

On this stage where you act out your roles,
These new parts are a challenge we know,
But you rehearse them each day and you learn,
That you'll soon learn your lines anyway.

So, when you're down and you're lost in the pit,
Just remember, to cope with your wit,
Let resilience and strength be your armour,
To get through and survive all the drama.

And although there are scenes that are testing,
Just removing your disguise and start resting,
Before long you'll see skies that are clearer,
And the light from the curtains gets nearer,

For the applause that you get
When you've done it,
Show that you've battled on
And then won it!

A Torch

There's a torch that glows and guides us,
Throughout our busy life.
A light that shines before us,
That's so hard to describe.

The one that dims our journey,
Sometimes when life is tough,
And takes us on steep pathways,
Where rocks we climb are rough.

Sometimes its power is weaker,
And other times so bright,
When cares we have are fewer,
And what's heavy, becomes light.

There's a spotlight for those times when,
Keeping focused is the key,
And the one that flashes for us,
When some things we cannot see.

Then when our body's weary,
From this life that we're found in,
It flickers down to soothe us,
So gently comforting.

It keeps on lighting pathways,
With our torch and all its power,
Guiding footsteps on life's journey,
Every second, minute, hour.

For until our job's accomplished,
Upon this place called earth,
Our torch will not extinguish,
From the moment of our birth.

Age

I won't be compliant when I get old,
Won't conform to the rules expected,
I won't wear the clothes that they sell in the shops,
That tell me my youth is rejected.

I'll keep wearing leggings, with hair straight and long,
I'll refuse to accept I'm declining,
I may even skateboard or wheelie on bikes,
And prefer noodle bars to fine dining.

I'll refuse all the drugs for lumbago,
Tell the doctor, I'll cure it myself,
I'll keep my limbs moving as pains come and go,
And refuse I've exceeded my shelf.

I will dance in the street if I want to,
Karaoke, even though I can't sing,
Be less occupied with reaction,
From others, it won't mean a thing.

Even when the inevitable wrinkles,
Are etched deep in my face, like a knife,
I'll hang on to ideas that are youthful,
And accept that there's more in this life.

And when the shell that holds me together,
May look like it's fading away,
My mind while it's got all its marbles,
Will live fully, with vigour, each day.

So, when others tell me I'm too old,
For the things that I did way back then,
I'll remind them, the old dog is still willing,
To learn new tricks and start over again!

Why Do I Feel 90?

Why do I feel 90?
When my mind feels 25?
My body's slowly giving up,
Although it's still alive.

My teeth are falling one by one,
Out of my ageing mouth.
And skin is wrinkly, all dried up,
With assets north and south.

Why is it that, although I speak,
With confidence, each day?
With most days losing keys and phone,
And small things go astray.

You see inside this middle-aged,
Worn out shell of little me,
Is a young energetic thing,
Who at heart is wild and free.

So, the theory is, if I believe,
I'm a young and vibrant chick,
I'll rejuvenate, feel vigorous,
And soon be very fit.

For age, while just a number thing,
And really in the mind,
I can think that I am really young,
I'll get off my behind.

And as I ponder on my pains and woes,
Declining physical ability,
I'll imagine that I'm fit and strong,
Equipped with fine agility.

And while my body does its thing,
Decaying by the minute,
I'll apply mind over matter still,
And imagine life's infinite.

Days

Days are where we live,
Houses we just borrow.
Think we own possessions,
But only till tomorrow.

Brand new cars and iPads,
Jewellery and gems.
Only ours for just a while,
Really just on lend.

We really don't own much at all,
It's hard to understand.
Leaving earth with empty hands,
Accumulations left on land.

So, when you're comparing others,
To yourself, just to impress,
Just remember that it doesn't mean,
That you have more and they have less.

For when ending comes a calling,
With possessions round your bed,
Remember that they all stay here,
There's no boasting when your dead!

Life is but a Gamble

Life is but a gamble,
A game of hit and miss.
The genes that we are born with,
That started with a kiss.

Some of us being lucky,
Bypassing all afflictions,
Avoiding bugs and sicknesses,
Despite of all addictions.

Drinking, smoking, parties,
Late nights and fatty food.
Living in denial,
With the lifestyle we've pursued.

As life slips right on by us,
Like a cat to catch its prey,
We survive with all our nine lives,
To live another day.

So live life with wild abandon,
Regardless of longevity.
As strict compliance with a virtuous life,
Can't insure against life's brevity.

For life is there for living,
And it just wouldn't be that right,
It we all chose to be clean living,
With our cocoa every night.

Let go of inhibitions,
Live life while you're still fit,
For time will pass, your youth will fade,
So, dance and sing don't quit.

Life's not about duration,
It's the quality that's key.
It's important to remember,
That we are truly free.

Give up procrastination,
And follow your desires,
Free yourself from all your fears,
And just see what transpires.

Don't Take Life Too Seriously

Don't take life too seriously,
You really do not need to,
Don't fret over all the things in life,
That hurt and make you blue.

For all things pass in time, we know,
Not easy to believe,
When life throws at us its garbage,
And we need to sit and grieve.

There's light around the corner,
When life may seem so dark,
There's no one out to get you,
Although right now it's stark.

And when the storms of life,
Have cleared to bring the sun,
You'll be surprised that you've got through,
And survived with battle won.

Dementia

Those wrinkles on her leathered frame,
Those bags beneath her eyes,
Those lines upon her frowning brow,
Hide memories that have died.

The past she had, not unlike yours,
Youth like the brightest star,
That blossoms as you travel on,
And makes you what you are.

Her mind filled now, with cotton wool,
Oblivious to the fact,
She brought you to this universe,
And survived for years, intact.

Those loves she's locked inside her head,
Yes, she once too, knew love,
You'll never know the history,
Of secrets, not for us.

To understand, that she knew then,
So much that passes by us,
When living in the daily grind,
With technology that binds us.

And now in her fragmented place,
With us just wondering how,
Her stories of a life once lived,
Locked in to hide, from now.

Saying Goodbye

When we say goodbye each morning,
To the ones we love and care,
Be just happy, to imagine,
That tomorrow they'll be there.

For each moment we spend judging,
Dwelling only on their faults,
Is another we are missing,
That cannot then be bought.

As the next day gives us newness,
Of a chance to make things right,
Grab the chance of opportunity,
To pack away the gripes.

To dispose of all the minute things,
Annoyances, fallouts,
Personality differences,
And harsh, unspoken doubts.

With tomorrow never promised,
And each minute, never known,
We can start with understanding,
Our superficial groans.

For when that moment's slipped before us,

There's no chance to start again,

And put behind those differences,

And then begin again.

So, remember, that this new day,

You can exercise the choice,

To unburden all the heaviness,

Of trivialities, unvoiced.

Then when the unexpected finds us,

And we've settled our discord,

They'll be no more wasted moments,

That in life, we can't afford.

Goodbyes

Goodbyes are never easy,
Some are bittersweet,
Some they mean forever,
Though in the future we might meet.

Some end romantic stories,
Of the sweet and fleeting kind,
And some, after a lifetime,
Of the paths of loves entwined.

Some may feel relief from,
Torment that lasted years,
For those who've been unlucky,
With the loves who've brought them tears.

So, with each farewell we have in life,
A new door opens up,
A new life, whatever that may mean,
And a chance to rise above.

For if there were no endings,
No chances to review,
Then our lives would be relentless,
With no hope to start anew.

The Art of Losing

The art of losing is hard to master,
Inevitable, as the day that turns to night,
To lose sight of dreams that hurt deep,
In the pit of an empty gut

And as simple as the hungry search for the
Only keys to your front door,
A habit familiar repetitive minor and major loss,
To never lose is to never start again

With new beginnings,
A lesson that irritates, angers and pains,
Revealing opportunities,
Yet unknown.

Yet burns like the branding iron,
Leaving familiar neural pathways,
Like the demise of an old friend,
Reminding of the impermanence of things, people and life.

Observing Humans

There are always opportunities to observe others and in doing so, we can never be bored. Most of these poems have been composed while 'waiting' and observing human behaviour.

Where Did the Rain Go?

Where did the rain go,
Was it sometime long ago?
When we avoided showers,
And the flowers they did grow.

Maybe it was April,
You know, all those months gone by,
When we put up bright umbrellas,
As dark clouds filled the sky.

Do we remember that complaining,
Like we do in the UK,
As we pulled on flowery wellies,
And our macs came out to play?

Now the heat's like global warming,
And we're melting with ice cream,
We all pray for just a downpour,
As the rain becomes a dream.

Random Acts of Kindness

I read today in the local press,
Of random acts of kindness,
In this troubled world, it's good to hear,
That these things still go on.

The woman who had lost her keys,
The man who paid your parking fee,
The child who opened the door for you,
The chap who let you jump the queue,

The checkout girl who hears our tales,
Of a troublesome week and all our ails,
In this troubled world, taken for granted,
The kindness seeds that still are planted.

Let's not let our faith be forgotten,
There's good out there, it's not all rotten.
It warms the heart, restores our trust
When all seems lost and we've cursed and cussed.

Just look around and you could find,
That others out there can be kind,
It's there to see and it's the finest,
These random acts of kindness.

Weather Talk

We talk about the weather,
Us here in the UK,
There's not a day that passes,
Where we don't have our say.

It happens in the bus queue,
When we're out for a jog,
Preoccupied with sun and rain,
The thunder and the fog.

This strange preoccupation,
Prompts us to discuss,
How we got drenched in downpours,
That made us curse and cuss.

We let it rule our movements,
Plan dates around the news,
That warn of us the darkest clouds,
And fill us with the blues.

Then when the sun is shining,
We venture from our homes,
With shorts and hats and sun specs,
All crowded in our drones.

'Let's catch a bit of colour,'
Those red as beetroots say,
Not bothered of the consequence,
We'll do it anyway.

And when our curtains close at night,
With the weather inclement,
We'll talk about tomorrow's plans,
And pray the sun is sent!

A & E

Broken limbs turn up on time,
Faces torn and twisted,
Pain etched in worn-out smiles,
Broken and unrested.

Feeble legs, like splintered wood,
Steady as they go,
Wobbling on a tightrope,
One puff and they will go.

Old and young they're bound up tight,
No freedom, like before,
Nature's goal to get them fixed,
So, they can move once more.

They call out names, as they go in,
Reluctantly like sheep do,
To do the things that pains them most,
Their expressions say they must go.

So out they come with sheet in hand,
With exercises nightly,
Or else they're looking forward to,
A life that's less than sprightly.

Miscommunication

Miscommunication,
You're texting once again,
No face to face for you at all,
You can't remember when.

All underlying messages,
With confusing texting speak,
The art of body language,
You've not seen it all week.

With painful gaps and pauses,
Not knowing why or when,
Assumptions made like solid facts,
And still, you try again.

Maybe they don't like me,
Never liked them anyway,
You're skilled at this mind reading,
You do it every day.

The art of conversation,
Just sitting face to face,
Extinct just like the laughing owl,
That's lost his rightful place.

So, miscommunication,
Don't lose the gift of speech,
As growth of life's technology,
Takes it further from our reach.

NHS

Doctors, healthcare workers,
Anaesthetists and nurses,
Working hard to heal the sick,
And paid from earners' purses.

Target-driven therapists,
Porters and midwives,
All right there to mend and cure,
And saving precious lives.

Surgeons donning scrub wear,
Fixing knees and hips and shoulders,
Plastic surgeons, lifting bits,
To prevent those getting older.

Occupational therapists,
Assisting those with needs,
And the voluntary services,
To listen, guide and feed.

Lifesaving cardiologists,
With skilled and slender hands,
Fit pacemakers and crafted valves,
And fibrillation bands.

Those dedicated paediatricians,
Healing sickness of our babies,
Health visitors in local schools,
Treating nits and fleas and scabies.

Ophthalmic eye technicians,
And those controlling pain,
Those cancer caring angels,
Their efforts not in vain.

So many more who care for us,
When illness comes to call,
Our saviour, that's the NHS,
Let's not see it fall.

Let's stand up for those they fought for,
Not just the privileged some,
When healthcare was a given,
And there for everyone.

For when it's taken over,
We'll look back in time to say,
That was the good old NHS,
And wish it could have stayed!

The Old UK

We never know just what to wear,
When weather turns from rain to fair,
One day it's cold, then baking hot,
Vacation plans, all go to pot.

One set of clothes, never enough,
Fill our cases until they're stuffed.
English breaks we choose to take,
While others across the water bake.

It seems we love the old UK,
And this is where many do stay,
Tents and rucksacks, off we go,
Cluttered motorways, kids in tow.

Land's End, Cornwall and Skegness,
The rain it pelts and we're a mess.
Caught in clouds, with no umbrellas,
Lining pockets of outdoor sellers.

As we are forced to purchase macs,
To keep the rain off all our backs,
But while we love the old UK,
We'll brave it all and here we'll stay.

The Beach

White capped waves the swell of summer,
Caressing bodies, white and parched,
Awaiting half-built sandy castles,
Where no soldiers ever marched.

Tanned beach sellers, heavily laden,
Anticipation in their eyes.
Weary arms carry their watches,
Others turn, with heavy sighs.

Clouds they pass, cooling the people,
Yet no one cares, as time stands still,
No concerns of solar damage,
As short-lived summers, go they will.

The captive sea, it pulls and welcomes,
All of those, seduced to dip,
Their toes to tempt them, with immersion,
Like kisses on a lover's lip.

Yet though the beach it stays consistent,
Canvas blank with crystal sea,
The scenes change daily as it welcomes
Others, after those who flee.

Bank Holiday Blues

Why can't the 31st of August
Bring us the morning sun?
Why can't it last all day for us,
Not rain on everyone?

Why are we all so hopeful,
On this late bank holiday?
That we'll get the chance to sun ourselves,
And the storms won't spoil our day.

Yet optimistic that we are,
Us people of our land,
We go to lengths to recreate,
Without the sea and sand.

Like rain dance gods we battle through,
Anticipation high.
Umbrellas, macs, drenched to the bone,
Prepare to keep us dry.

Acceptance order of the day,
Taking what we get,
Some prefer to stay at home,
With duvet and boxset.

So, bank holiday blues, you won't deter,
Us folk with hardy souls,
It's in our genes to take it all,
Wet feet and soggy rolls!

Just on this Bus

This bus, a carriage for the carless
Empty upstairs, the driver
Playing his childhood game of picking up passengers
Like the 'wheels on the bus'.

Me, conversing with a masked woman
Muffled words prompting empathic nods
About missing, about loneliness, about life
Just moments of speaking

Breaking the boredom of lockdown
In temporary connections
Meaningful and meaningless
Just beginning, to be familiar again

With the art of speaking,
The art of listening,
Just on this journey,
Just on this bus.

Humour

These 'tongue in cheek' poems have come about from observing the changing times that we live in, mostly comparing how things used to be in 'the old days'.

Meat and Potatoes Only

No peri sauce or noodles,
No fancy rice with cheese,
No chilli peppered chicken,
No frozen spuds for ease.

No chocolate jam-filled doughnuts,
No blueberry flavoured buns,
No infused pork wrapped parcels,
Or schnitzels in breadcrumbs.

For way back in the old days.
When we were just small fry,
No money for these fancies,
There was for us to buy.

Instead we lived more hand to mouth,
Just three square meals a day,
We ate when we were hungry,
With fish once on Friday.

With veg all fresh from gardens,
And meat all locally sourced,
Little then leftover,
So, no fussiness of course.

What of any weight problems?
No slimming clubs or gym,
Was riding on our bicycles,
And walking kept us thin.

No cars to pick up shopping,
Just the delivery man,
Who called fortnightly Monday,
When we queued outside his van.

A mini supermarket,
With all the stuff we'd need,
From margarine to cooked sliced meat,
For mouths, there were to feed.

No wonder that we're so confused,
And spend so much precious time,
In crowded supermarkets,
A standing in a line.

The choices, oh too many,
That clutter heads so vastly,
With unnecessary produce,
And ingredients so ghastly.

Stuff for every dietary need,
And meals just for the lonely,
Oh, please just let's have them back,
Meat and potatoes only!

Bacon Sandwich Blues

What happened to the transport café,
In the high street we once knew?
Now I look and find to my dismay,
There's not even a few.

Those coffee bars with posh new names.
The others cordon bleu,
Serve half the portions fancied up,
You even have to queue.

They're others who profess to know,
The tastes of all the many.
I look around for transport cafés,
Alas there are not any.

You know the ones that served a brew,
To builders and the others.
To hard-up folk who took along,
Their sisters, mum and brothers

No bacon rolls with cups of tea,
Milkshakes made like they used to.
Those kids blew bubbles through their straws,
You know the ones, now don't you?

The homemade pies with mushy peas
And custard-coated crumbles,
With breakfasts big, with toast for free,
I heard nobody grumble.

So now they've disappeared from sight,
With the others that they choose.
I'll never quit till I see again.
I've got bacon sandwich blues!

Healthy Words of Wisdom

Watch your weight they tell us,
Go easy on your liver,
Eat kale mashed up with beetroot,
And cheese, but just a sliver.

Opt for decaffeination,
Substituting with red bush,
Juice, seasonal blood orange,
That burns fat from round your tush.

Steam veg instead of boiling,
As we'll kill off all the minerals,
Or be scolded by the diet police,
Who preach to us like criminals.

Make sure we get our eight hours sleep,
Or we'll shorten up our life,
Age before we're due to,
Or succumb under the knife.

Be sure to cut out sugar,
As you may become diabetic,
Opt for distilled water,
That makes you feel pathetic.

Then after all this good advice,
Don't forget to pound the street,
After consuming wholemeal pasta,
And the right amount of meat.

And if this is too much for us,
Too boring or contrived,
Then stuff your face with what you like,
And no doubt you'll still survive!

Laugh

Just laugh for no reason,
See how it makes you feel,
You don't need to watch a comedy,
To chuckle like a seal.

Don't worry about others,
Who'll think you're rather strange,
When tears are streaming down your face,
When you're not acting your age.

Don't take life so cautiously,
Just chuckle, laugh and chortle,
There's enough in life that's serious,
We're really not immortal.

Just find all opportunities,
In the midst of all the gloom,
To find something that tickles you,
To lift you from the doom.

And soon you'll see that once you do,
Your laughter will be caught,
By others, who'll appreciate,
The joy your laughter brought.

Recycling

Don't throw your junk in the bin please,
Just wash all your margarine tubs
Avoid squashing your cereal boxes,
Do the Blue Peter thing that you loved

Cut greeting cards up with some scissors
And transform into fancy gift tags,
Which you can store in the old biscuit tin now
And recycle your old plastic bags.

Put tea leaves around your tomatoes
And spud peelings upon your green beans
Use those empty spring water bottles
To divert all the cats from your greens.

And then if you've got time to just do this
Rinse all of your tins, sparkling sweet
Then thread through some string, like you used to
And then walk on the cans with your feet.

So, this weekend, think foraging mushrooms
Using scraps from leftovers for lunch
And buy hens that lay eggs almost daily
Eaten on brown bread for brunch.

With the time you've got with your smartphone,
Take some snaps of the family and kids,
Then create a designer photo frame,
Out of all of your margarine lids.

Then when you wake from your recycling nightmare
And return to your normal lifestyle,
You'll continue to throw all in the same bin
And risk a fine from the council you fear!

Stuff

Why accumulate stuff,
That clutters up our brain?
Cupboards spewing out with it,
We've overspent again.

Why not chuck it in the bin?
Or throw it out the door?
Or better still don't purchase it
And bring it home no more!

Coffee Shop

We're all a nation of addicts,
In every sense of the word
With thousands of types of fresh coffee
And some that are simply absurd.

With a double shot, white cappuccino
And a chocolate, mocha divine.
A vanilla infused 'cappamachi'
With a dollop of cream and white wine.

Have you heard of a frothy marmito?
Maybe try one when you're out with a mate,
Just like its namesake, we all know well,
It's one that you'll love, or you'll hate.

Have you encountered a one-shot ice blaster?
Flavoured mostly with brandy and thyme,
Goes down well with a scoop of gelato
And a dash of liquor and lime.

There's also the half-fat 'pacchino',
Enhanced with fructose and mint,
More expensive that those on the menu,
The barista will give you a hint.

And just when you thought you had finished,
While the froth's sitting fresh on your lip,
You'll be landed the bill on your table,
That didn't include the big tip!

Peace & War

No matter how old we are, we have known about or experienced war, even though war is out of our control, we can make small differences to hopefully find the antidote: peace. These poems come from deep reflections on recent world events and some not so recent.

Listen to the Silence

Listen to the silence,
Listen to its sound,
For peace and all its beauty,
Is so good to be around.

Do not take for granted,
The stillness so enchanting,
Like flowers, that grow up from the soil,
And blossom from their planting.

For silence is short lived,
Its presence comes and goes,
With conflict in the world today,
Creating highs and lows.

The wars that never stop out there,
That interrupt its flow,
And the fine line that divides it,
For some will never know.

So, listen while it's silent,
Let the nation softly sleep,
Before we are at war again,
Woke up from slumber deep.

Still

When the stillness of peace is upon us
And the wars and the terror have passed
Will they know of the damage and horror
That the sorrows and sadness will last?

Will their morals give way to submission
As they see that it's wasted and futile?
Or fight on with such cowardly protest
And continue with attacks that are so vile?

When they're old and reflecting on actions,
Will their conscience be pricked by such shame?
Or will hearts that are hardened with hatred,
Continue to hurt, kill and maim?

So still are the moments between which,
We live and pretend we are brave,
As they sit planning death and destruction,
With their minds twisted, sick and depraved.

If Only

What if love meant no more wars?
No conflict, hate or crime,
What if love meant we all lived at peace,
Each day would be divine.

If for only just one full day,
Each human being ceased hating,
They'd tolerate each other's views,
And be accommodating.

So, if only just for one full day,
We'd send love to all the others,
Matching actions with our words
All nations, sisters, brothers.

The dream of this utopia,
In this world of 'if only' notion,
Lies only in the idealist,
Believing love's the potion.

But love for all's impossible,
For those indoctrinated,
Who cannot see the damage done,
To those who are so hated.

So, roses blood red, as they are,
We'll give to friends and lovers,
Even though in this big world,
There's blood shed for the others.

So, take a moment, spare a thought.
For those who'll never know,
The power of love and all it means,
To fill with hope and grow.

For love in all its many forms,
Mends scars, ends wars and pain,
And all we do, is do our bit,
With hatred we refrain.

Yes, love's the only antidote,
The method, fix and cure,
For all the sufferings in the world,
That they so do endure.

Poppies Round the Tower

Poppies round the tower,
Blood red like what was shed,
Each one to symbolise a life,
That lived and then fell dead.

Poppies round the tower,
Their beauty, more than haunting,
Evoke such thoughts and fill the heart,
Of war, so cruel and daunting.

Poppies round the tower,
Relations, yours and mine,
Their lives so short, their fight so long,
Their courage so sublime.

Poppies round the tower,
The tears that flow because,
They've gone to somewhere far from earth,
And left behind their loss.

Poppies round the tower,
Remember them with pride,
For now, they rest with no more pain,
With angels by their side.

As the Sun Goes Down

As our daytime turns to dusk,
On this Remembrance Day,
We'll remember them with pride,
As the sun goes down.

As we go about our daily lives,
They're never far away,
From the legacy, they left behind,
As the sun goes down.

As we tread each steady footprint,
On the paths that they once trod,
We'll reflect on how they toiled and fought,
As the sun goes down.

As we look upon this England,
With the freedom, that we have,
We'll bless them with our grateful hearts,
As the sun goes down.

The World Cries

The world cries with rain.
It sobs for your loss.
It opens its nimbus clouds and pours your tears of pain on our still
ground.
It feels the terror of your people,
And spills out the chills,
Of your frozen bones.
It weeps for you and your loved ones
And the sorrow of your unending grief and pain.
Still you fight on,
You fight for your family, freedom and your loved ones,
Your liberty, your values and for love,
For peace, for safety and for your future,
And while the sky and the air fills with the smoke
And fire of the bombings and heavy blasts
And when your blood spills out onto the streets
Still, you fight on.
You are as relentless as those who try to overtake you and those,
Who pull you down and destroy your lives, your spirit, your
determination.
And as the world cries for you, it watches on in helplessness,
It wants to wrap you up in its clouds of sadness
And pour peace upon you and your broken lands
And the world cries with you.

Let's Remember

Let's remember as we recall,
Those we knew who were to fall.
Two events that changed the world,
As lives before them were unfurled

Lives so precious children left.
Wives and lovers all bereft.
Two events though years apart,
Pull the strings upon the heart.

Ground zero and world war two,
Circumstance it wasn't you.
Poppies strewn like they were blood
And towers fell down beneath the mud.

Pointless suffering, beyond compare,
Thousands lost with such despair.
The lives, the loves, the people maimed,
And depth of pain they all sustained.

For what we ask as we remember,
Families left and lives dismembered.
The war relentless, all for what?
To start again like we forgot.

And yet, until they'll all agree,
That all we need to make us free,
To live our lives, not judge others,
Respect for life and one another.

Fighting back achieves so little.
Just makes us cold and hard and brittle.
So, while they think of their solution,
They'll just continue, revolution.

Our Fellow Human Beings

Bless those poor souls seeking safety, without shelter,
Clinging relentlessly in tears, with all their life,
The innocent and frightened, denied language,
Escaping terrors in their countries, filled with strife.

Reaching out with hands so strong, just wanting freedom,
At the mercy of this land, so rich compared,
To their homes from which they flee so cold and spartan,
Begging us for the help with such despair

Not deserving how they're treated, frail and helpless.
Wanting peace and shelter, they're denied.
Nobody knows what they can do to help them
And while they wait behind the gates, their children died.

So, as they flock like distressed sheep across our borders
Let's reach out to help our fellow human beings,
For it's just chance we're all safe inside this country
And being in their shoes, is just in our bad dreams.

Seasons

All seasons have their own beauty and autumn and winter are my favourites. Christmas is a time that brings mixed feelings for many of us and this section captures the air of cynicism and sadness, as well as the magic of the seasons.

Autumn

Autumn winds bring out the people,
Dust the cobwebs from their leathered feet,
Put the boots on, heels need mending,
Pounding feet press downward on littered street.

Leaves floating, dropping slowly,
Sadly dying, summer's gone,
With the starkness of the branches,
Where their elegance once shone.

Rustling now amongst the dirt,
Feet trampling on earths' terrain,
Swept and recycled crudely,
Until we watch nature's cycle breathe again.

Autumn Change

There's a hint of winter in the air,
Sun sitting low in the sky,
The last of the autumn blackberries,
Shrivelled, now ready to die.

The night air filled with Applewood kindling,
Being burnt in their houses so snug,
Rosy cheeks coming home from hardworking,
Now cocooned in a warming bear hug.

There's a sadness that's left as the night falls,
And the mercury falls like the leaves,
But that's nature and yearly it happens,
As we say goodbye and we grieve.

So like life, so the cycle continues,
As the seasons unfold like our lives,
There's no room on this world for forever,
As we witness and nature survives.

So, embracing the spring and the summer,
The autumn and winter so chilled,
If nothing died on this planet there's nothing,
Without the warmth and the challenge of change.

Freedom

Stepping from your doorway,
Feeling warmth upon your face,
Or the coolness of the autumn,
Anticipates winter's embrace.

Watching white-winged creatures,
Flying south, all passport free,
And wishing that us humans,
Could soar sometimes to flee.

So, trapped inside our circumstance,
With life that so restricts,
Imagination takes us to,
A life that we depict.

So, freedom lives inside our head,
Yet escapes when it allows,
Indulged in nature's given gift,
Soaring high up in the clouds.

Halloween

31st of October,
That spooky time of year,
When cowering in the darkness,
They shudder with such fear.

The ghouls and night-time zombies,
Arising from the ground,
Return to earth to terrorise,
Those who dare to be found.

The ghosts with white drawn faces,
The haunted fiendish few,
The living dead that lurk beneath,
The earth cooks eyeball stew.

And right behind the tombstones,
The grim reaper in disguise,
Torments all those who enter in,
With bloodcurdling piercing eyes.

Yes, fear lurks there awaiting,
For those who shudder and fear,
All in the imagination,
Only at this time of year.

Till dawn arises after,
The spooks have gone to sleep,
Back to a place where no one knows,
The otherworldly deep.

Winter

As the mercury keeps falling,
The reluctant people show their seasonal attire.
Colours lighting up the looming, winter sky,
With a backdrop of falling leaves,

Only to have their beauty kicked
And swept, with their others.
Coating the slippery pathways,
With a spectacle of colour.

The dew glistening, with its temporary morning glow
Awaits those, who tread, with worn-down boots,
Or those who dare, with bunion laden feet,
In unserviceable shoes.

Walking like the toddler, without their mother's hand.
Wobbling, tripping, balancing,
Being a well-earned skill,
Concentration etched on their faces.

The stillness of the blackened evening sky,

Sending souls to hibernate behind heated walls

Faces lacklustre from the absence of solar rays

And waists that expand full of sponge puddings

Empty bellies and voids,

That cannot fill,

The hunger of winter's call.

Christmas Decorations

As I go through these decorations,
Memories come to mind,
Of winter days and laughter,
Of my very favourite kind.

These boxes filled with so much love,
The tinsel old and worn,
Fill me with a warming glow,
When my tree I do adorn.

The worn and grubby Santa,
The tree that's past its date,
The silver baubles that once were bright,
Are still just as ornate.

If only I could go back in time,
To capture all those days,
Then I'd tell all those that I once knew,
And they would be amazed.

I'd tell them how whilst time has passed,
In this world now they're gone,
That some things in life will never change,
And memories linger on.

Now every time I find this box,
And go back to the past,
I'll realise that while some things fade,
That love will always last.

Cynic's Christmas

As the sun sets over the uneven landscape,
The people rush on,
Heads filled with forgotten tasks,
Christmas amnesia hits at last.

List on list in pockets on phones,
Stored in a network, amongst,
A pond-like brain,
That's infested with the fever of festivity.

Excitement blunted through a swamp of societal expectations,
'We must have this, they need that,'
Credit cards swiping the machines like passing money branches,
That break in January.

'Wait, there's another fool,' you and me,
Caught up in robotic form,
Scooping up items with familiar hysteria,
Items that when the season's past, return to grace, the bending shelves.

Ensconced in robotic automation,
Bowing to the demands of the psychological geniuses,
That prey on us sentimental fools,
Emptying our purses, like a pickpocket's dream.

But then the excitement of the children's faces,
Like you and I, in years long gone,
All worth the pain, the anguish and empty pockets,
To see their innocence before the hand of cynicism comes.

Christmas Fever

It's Christmas fever once again,
There is no vaccination,
To shield us from its viral power,
We succumb with fascination.

The symptoms heat our body through,
Our temperature starts rising,
Expectations to purchase gifts,
For others, we're surprising.

The medication, is to buy,
Though side effects expected,
When gazing into piggy banks,
And credit cards rejected.

With little option to escape,
We deny it's around the corner,
We'll all succumb sooner or later,
And for many it's such trauma.

So, when you see those baubles bright,
And Santa shouting 'ho ho'
It's time to just accept it's here,
Or get right out and go go.

And if you do decide to stay,
Just expect you'll catch the virus,
For Jingle Bells and Auld Lang Syne,
Will surely seek and find us.

For soon this time will pass and go,
And we'll soon be feeling brighter,
With gifts that we will never use,
And pockets so much lighter!

Festive Smiles

Put up the festive lights now,
It's Christmas time once more,
Time to decorate the tree,
Put wreaths upon the door.

Forget our normal routine,
It's time for us to indulge,
No thoughts of January,
When we'll battle with the bulge.

Smiling brightly at each other,
For this is what we do,
I don't know why we do this,
I haven't got a clue.

When from New Year until November,
We will barely crack a smile,
Avoiding all eye contact,
In the supermarket aisle.

So, extend our Christmas spirit,
For twelve months through the year,
We shouldn't need December,
To greet everyone with cheer.

A smile will go a long way,
And it's always there for free,
Not wrapped in fancy paper,
Around the Christmas tree.

So, when others make eye contact,
And smile with nodding head,
Don't turn away like always,
Just return the smile instead.

Who knows what joy that this will bring,
For the ripples of goodwill,
Will warm the heart of others,
Unloved, in pain or ill.

Christmas is for giving,
Not all that's good costs money,
For when smiles are shared with strangers,
We'll be lifted with harmony.

Capture

Capture the magic of Christmas,
Keep each passing moment to mind,
Feel the warmth as it melts all our troubles,
And be grateful at what we'll then find.

If we've family and friends, try to be with them,
Or to speak on the phone if that's all,
There'll be memories to make when we're sharing,
Building pictures, we'll later recall.

Keep in mind there are wars and such sorrows,
That we're richer than what we're believing,
Being grateful whatever we're given,
And kind to those others who're grieving.

Play games, those old ones we've forgotten.
The ones that bring people together,
They'll bring laughter and good conversation,
And jokes, we'll remember forever.

Put away cares for this moment,
And if there are troubles with health,
Just join hands, round your table, with loved ones,
As these times mean so much more than wealth.

And when Christmas is finally over,
When the turkey and tinsel are tattered,
We'll look back at those magical moments,
And know we did all that so mattered.

A Christmas Poem

No snowflakes from the window,
No ice upon the ground,
I wonder from my window,
Where Christmas can be found.

Not in the drunken revellers,
Nor in the bustling shops,
Where shoppers huddle round the tills,
And the banks who pull their stops.

The meaning of this time of year,
Is lost beneath all this,
The hustle bustle madness,
Conceal treasures we all miss.

The family time that we all knew,
As huddled round a fire,
When we sang songs of the festive kind,
That we all so desired.

When sacks were filled with simple things,
That enthralled and filled our heart,
The magic of each Christmas time,
Built memories we impart.

The simplicity of those past times,
When Christmas had such meaning,
When children woke with sleepy eyes,
From their twilight world of dreaming.

Where every toy and colouring book,
Was ours to keep and treasure,
Well-loved and read, with joy each day,
With those we loved, beyond all measure.

For memories stay, so give thanks that we,
All know the power of sharing,
When we all learnt the power of love,
Through simplicity and caring.

Memories of Christmas

I can hear those church bells ringing,
Feel the cold crisp winter's air,
As Christmas Day approaches,
Can't believe it's been a year.

Twelve months have been so busy,
And just like the film we saw,
Four weddings and a funeral,
Tears of joy and so much more.

It's hard sometimes for others,
And often comes to all,
That we miss loved ones we've shared with,
Who we cannot see or call.

As memories fill our senses,
Of the days with them we shared,
Especially at this time of year,
We remember, how they cared.

Even though they can't be with us,
Sharing joy this festive time,
Our memory takes us right back then,
To recall those days so fine.

So, as we join in celebrations,
With those absent from our home,
We'll recall those moments, happy times,
And know that we're not alone.

For whatever you believe in,
You can know, they'll never leave,
In our hearts, they are still living,
So, no need to fret or grieve.

And if you believe that there's a heaven,
There's a place inside your mind,
That in the arms of Christmas angels,
They'll reside at this festive time.

So, enjoy all those days with loved ones,
Whether that be girl or boy,
For all the days spent making memories,
Looking back will bring such joy.

Early Christmas Merchandise

It's true I am a humbug,
And some things I would prefer,
The selling of Christmas merchandise,
In September, I'd deter.

We've just got over Easter,
And autumn's barely here.
The practice of early shopping,
With Christmas, nowhere near.

It really is perplexing,
With so many birthdays due,
That 'normal' cards are now not seen,
And choices are so few.

I asked the shop assistant,
Where are the others please?
She looks me right back in the eye,
As if I'd spoken Chinese.

Maybe I'm the minority,
As it seems, this is the thing,
To be prepared well in advance,
Easing financial sting.

Now I'll jump down off my soap box,
Get out my Santa hat,
Get in the mood, be a Christmas dude
Eat humble pie, get fat!

New Year

The new year has just begun,
We've had our share of trouble,
Let's face it with a brand-new start,
And leave behind the rubble,
For what has past, has long since gone,
No point in dwelling on and on,
Things that can no more be altered,
No matter how we tripped and faltered,
Mistakes were made and lives were shattered,
So, don't continue to be battered,
The new year prompts a chance, a reason,
To start January, a brand-new season,
To forgive, let go, to heal, to rest,
And let this new year be the best!

'When the cogs on the wheel of life get rusty, take them apart and work on each with care… just one step at a time.'

J A Scott